W9-BEJ-774

JACKIE
JOYNER
KERSEE

JACKIE JOYNER KERSEE

SUPERWOMAN

Margaret J. Goldstein
and
Jennifer Larson

Lerner Publications Company
Minneapolis

For Lea, who loved to run

First Avenue Editions,
an imprint of Lerner Publishing Group
241 First Avenue North
Minneapolis, MN 55401 U.S.A.

Website address: www.lernerbooks.com

Library of Congress Cataloging-in-Publication Data

Goldstein, Margaret J.
  Jackie Joyner-Kersee : superwoman / Margaret J. Goldstein and
Jennifer Larson
    p. cm. — (The Achievers)
    Summary: Chronicles the life of the track and field star who has
had medal-winning performances in three Olympics.
    ISBN 0-8225-0524-X (lib. bdg. : alk. paper)
    ISBN 0-8225-9653-9 (pbk. : alk. paper)
    1. Joyner-Kersee, Jacqueline, 1962–   —Juvenile literature.
2. Track and field athletes—United States—Biography—Juvenile lit-
erature.   3. Women track and field athletes—United States—
Biography—Juvenile literature. [1. Joyner-Kersee, Jacqueline, 1962–
2. Track and field athletes.   3. Afro-Americans—Biography.]
I. Larson, Jennifer. II. Title. III. Series.
GV697.J69G65 1994
796.42'092—dc20
[B]   93-2976

Copyright © 1994 by Lerner Publications Company

All rights reserved. International copyright secured. No part of this book may be
reproduced, stored in a retrieval system, or transmitted in any form or by any means—
electronic, mechanical, photocopying, recording, or otherwise—without the prior
written permission of Lerner Publications Company, except for the inclusion
of brief quotations in an acknowledged review.

Manufactured in the United States of America
8 9 10 11 12 13 – JR – 07 06 05 04 03 02

Contents

Jackie Joyner-Kersee went to Barcelona looking for gold.

1

World's Greatest

Jackie Joyner-Kersee surged down the track at the Estadi Olimpic—the Olympic Stadium—in Barcelona, Spain. The 5-foot, 10-inch, 153-pound athlete pumped her powerful arms and legs. She held a narrow lead in the 200-meter race—one of seven track-and-field events in a grueling, two-day contest called the heptathlon.

Jackie's rivals dashed with her toward the finish line. Each woman hoped to shave fractions of a second from her time at the tape. Each strained for the lead.

As the pack rounded the curve of the track, Bob Kersee, Jackie's coach and husband, held his breath. If Jackie slowed or stumbled at the curve, her hopes for a gold medal in the heptathlon would be lost.

Jackie Joyner-Kersee was one of the top athletes in the world. She owned the world record in the heptathlon. She had earned two gold medals at the

Olympic Games in Seoul, South Korea, four years before and was expected to win another here at the 1992 Games.

Yet, competing in the heptathlon at the 1991 Track and Field World Championships in Japan, Jackie had fallen during the 200-meter race. She had pulled the hamstring in her right leg and had dropped to the ground in pain. Running the same race at the 1992 Olympic Trials in New Orleans, Jackie nearly fell again. "She's afraid in the 200 now," Bob Kersee explained after the trials. "Her ghost tapped her on the shoulder."

But there were no ghosts on this day, Saturday, August 1, 1992. Jackie was unbeatable. She powered through the curve in the 200 without a hitch and flew toward the finish line with a winning time.

The slim lead she had established over her opponents earlier in the day—with good showings in the 100-meter hurdles, high jump, and shot put—now swelled to a hefty margin. The lead only grew larger as Jackie tackled Sunday's events—the long jump, javelin throw, and 800-meter run—like a master.

When the final marks were tallied, none of her rivals was even close. Any heptathlete who had hoped to take the gold medal away from reigning champion Jackie Joyner-Kersee would have to wait another four years. With her victory, she became the only multi-sport athlete other than American

Bob Mathias—the 1948 and 1952 decathlon champion—to win back-to-back gold medals at the Olympic Games.

Like all the great superheroes, Jackie can fly!

Runners must clear 10 hurdles in the 100-meter hurdle race.

At the conclusion of the 800 meters, Jackie quietly left the track to take a rest. The crowd in the stadium, however, wasn't ready to see her leave. "JACKIE, JACKIE," the fans shouted. They wouldn't let up until she came back and took a victory lap. "I was tired," Jackie said, "but when they started calling me, I had to take that victory lap and shake hands with those people."

"Hardly anyone ever watches the heptathlon," Jackie said modestly. "I never thought that [the chant] would happen to me."

If Jackie was modest about her fame, others were not so shy. Jackie Joyner-Kersee has been called many things: the World's Greatest Female Athlete, Superwoman, and the First Lady of Sports. Bruce Jenner, the 1976 Olympic decathlon champion, described her no less grandly in Barcelona. She's "the best who's ever lived," said Jenner.

Many sportswriters say Jackie is the world's greatest athlete—male *or* female!

Jackie strengthened both her mind and her body at Lincoln High in
East St. Louis.

2
Revving Up

Track-and-field coach George Ward waited near the long jump pit behind his house in East St. Louis, Illinois. One of Ward's young long jumpers was late for practice. Meanwhile, 12-year-old Jackie Joyner, a skinny neighborhood girl with pigtails, played around the sand-filled pit. She wanted to take a jump. As Ward looked on, Jackie took off down the runway and soared over the sand.

When Jackie landed, Coach Ward was stunned. He measured her jump by the mark her shoes left in the sand. Nearly 17 feet. Most *high school* athletes couldn't jump that far. Jackie jumped again. This time she sailed even farther!

Few people were surprised to hear that Jackie Joyner had landed a king-size long jump. Jackie was already well known in East St. Louis for her speed on the track. In fact, Jackie had been leading the pack for years.

When Jacqueline Joyner was born, on March 3, 1962, her grandmother Evelyn had predicted that the new baby would be "the first lady of something" someday. So Jackie was named after the nation's First Lady at the time, Jacqueline Kennedy.

Evelyn's prediction was right from the start. Young Jackie seemed to excel at everything she did. At the Mary E. Brown Community Center near her home, Jackie danced and acted in plays. She played basketball and led cheers for other teams. "One day they put a sign out for track," she remembers. "So, I figured I could try this, too."

Jackie was nine when she entered her first race. She lost—but she kept running. She trained hard and improved her technique. The coaches at the community center encouraged Jackie's talents and helped her enter track meets against kids from other towns. Soon, Jackie was bringing home trophies.

By age 12, Jackie was faster than most of the boys in her neighborhood—including her 14-year-old brother, Al. "My dad teased me because Jackie was always so good," Al remembers. "She could jump farther, and she was fast."

To practice jumping, Jackie built her own long jump pit. She and her little sisters, Angela and Debra, filled potato chip bags with sand from a neighborhood park. They dug a pit at home and, bag by bag, they filled the pit with sand.

Most athletes pour their energy into one or two specialties—but not Jackie. She was an all-around athlete with powerful legs and a strong upper body. Her talents seemed limitless: she could run, jump, and throw. Coaches from the community center introduced Jackie to the pentathlon—a five-event contest consisting of the long jump, 100-meter hurdles, high jump, shot put, and 800-meter run. Jackie did well in all of them!

"A coach told us that it's good to be able to be versatile," Jackie recalls. "Because when you want to make an Olympic team there are so many sprinters, jumpers, and throwers, but there are not a lot of people who can do so many different events. That's when I decided to do the pentathlon."

Jackie wanted to compete in the Olympic Games. For a while, though, she would have to be content with the Junior Olympics. This program, sponsored by the Amateur Athletic Union (AAU), brings together the best young athletes in the nation.

Jackie's opponents were tough and so was her training. "If not for the Junior Olympics," Jackie believes, "I might not have been able to develop into a top-notch athlete."

At age 15, Jackie won the AAU's national junior pentathlon championship. (She took the title four years in a row.) *Sports Illustrated* magazine noted her achievement and printed Jackie's picture in its "Faces in the Crowd" column about outstanding amateur athletes.

Jackie was proud. She was serious about track. But traveling to distant cities for track meets took money, and Jackie's family didn't have much money to spare. Even food was scarce. Sometimes Jackie ate only a mayonnaise sandwich for lunch. She often wore the same dress to school day after day—it was all she had.

"We were not a poor family," Jackie is quick to point out, "but a family that had a lot of loving and caring in it. I knew that eventually, if we continued to do things right, something good was going to happen."

Jackie worked to pay her own way to track meets. She sold candy bars to her friends and neighbors and earned money for trips to national competitions as far away as Yakima, Washington.

Jackie's parents, Alfred and Mary, gave their four children money when they could. Mary Joyner worked as a nurse's aide in a local hospital. Alfred held a job two hours away from home as a railroad switch operator. He could only see his family on weekends— but steady work close to home was hard to come by. There weren't many good jobs available in East St. Louis.

The city was poor and it was rough. Jackie once saw a man murdered on her street. All around her neighborhood, Jackie saw poverty and violence. She planned to make a better life for herself when she grew up. Sports would help her get there.

"I never despaired," she said. "I always had something to shoot for each year—to jump just one inch farther.

"I kept saying to myself, 'I've got to work hard, I've got to be successful.'"

Jackie's brother, Al, remembers making a vow during childhood. "Someday we were going to make it," he said. "Make it out [of poverty]. Make it different."

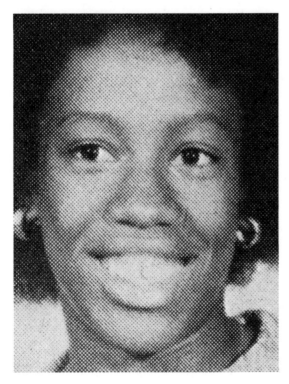

As a teenager, Jackie ran with a track club called the East St. Louis Railers.

Much of Jackie's inspiration to succeed came from her mother. Mary Joyner insisted that her children attend church and concentrate on their schoolwork.

Mary had had her first child at age 16 and had dropped out of school to raise her family. She didn't want her own daughters to become teenage mothers too. She wanted them to stay in school and stay away from boys. Mrs. Joyner wouldn't let Jackie attend high school dances or date at all.

"As the oldest girl, everything came down hardest on me," Jackie remembers. "I couldn't date boys until I was 18. There was no debate over it. So I just lost myself in school and sports."

"She just went at it," Jackie's father remembers. "She was always up at 5 A.M., running."

At Lincoln High School in East St. Louis, Jackie ran track and played basketball and volleyball. With Jackie on board, the Lincoln High girls basketball team beat its opponents by an average of 53 points per game! Jackie Joyner "is the finest athlete in the state of Illinois," one sportswriter marveled after watching her on the basketball court.

Jackie was dominant on the track too. During her junior year, she set an Illinois high school record with a long jump of 20 feet, 7½ inches. She won national junior long jump titles two years in a row.

Al was also a powerful jumper. During his senior year at Lincoln High, he placed third in the state in

18

the triple jump event. He eventually won a track scholarship to Arkansas State University.

The Joyners were bound for the top. In 1980 the U.S. Olympic Committee invited Jackie to try out for the Olympic long jump team. She was just a senior in high school!

At the 1980 Olympic Trials, Jackie competed against the best long jumpers in the United States. She didn't jump well enough to win a spot on the U.S. team—she took eighth place—but track-and-field coaches from across the country took notice of this promising young newcomer.

Despite her busy sports schedule, Jackie never neglected her studies. She earned good grades and prepared for college. Lincoln High track coach Nino Fennoy believed that Jackie would succeed off the athletic field as well as on it. He encouraged her to polish her grammar, writing, and speaking skills. "Where you're going," Coach Fennoy told Jackie, "you'll need to express yourself with more than your legs and arms."

Jackie graduated in 1980 in the top 10 percent of her class. She had two goals in mind: a college education and a spot on the 1984 Olympic team. Many colleges offered Jackie scholarships. But one school topped the list for both academics and athletic training: the University of California at Los Angeles (UCLA).

"I always wanted to go to UCLA," Jackie remembers.

Jackie looked up to sprinter Evelyn Ashford (left), who went on from UCLA to win four Olympic gold medals.

"I watched them win the [women's] national basketball championship in 1978, and I also knew that Evelyn Ashford was from UCLA. The name just kept popping up all the time."

The coaches at UCLA were equally excited about having the gifted young athlete from East St. Louis attend their school. The university offered Jackie a basketball scholarship. She was off to Los Angeles.

3
Ready for Takeoff

At UCLA Jackie threw herself into sports and schoolwork. The university had plenty to offer: top-level coaching, warm weather for training, students from around the world, and challenging classes. Jackie felt homesick at first, but she enjoyed college.

Jackie had been at UCLA for only one semester when she received terrible news. Her mother, Mary, had developed a brain disease called meningitis. Both Jackie and Al hurried home from college.

When Jackie arrived home, she heard more bad news. Mary was "brain-dead," the doctors explained. She had fallen into a coma and would never recover.

Jackie and Al gathered with their father and sisters and made a painful decision. They asked the doctors to turn off the life-support machines that kept their mother alive. "If we had left her on the machines," Jackie says, "she'd never have known us, and she would have continued suffering indefinitely."

Running helped Jackie through hard times.

Mary's death devastated the whole family. Jackie was depressed and didn't feel like going back to school. But she knew her mother wouldn't want her to quit. "With her gone," Jackie explained, "some of her determination passed to me.

"I felt that I was the strong link. If I went back to school and did what I was supposed to do, everyone else [in the family] would know, 'Hey—we're not supposed to sit here and cry. Jackie's going to get on with her life, and we should too.'"

Back in Los Angeles, an assistant track coach, Bob Kersee, offered Jackie his friendship. "He said if I had doubts and needed to talk them out," Jackie remembers, "I could come to him. He had lost his mother [as a teenager] too. He let me know he cared about me as a person as well as an athlete."

Jackie Joyner and Bob Kersee became close friends. Bob watched Jackie fly across the long jump pit. He saw her tear up the basketball court as a starting forward for the UCLA Bruins. "From the first day I saw Jackie," Bob says, "I knew she was the greatest woman athlete I'd ever seen."

Bob was worried though. As a pentathlete, Jackie was strong in some events but weak in others. Bob thought she would do better with a different training program. "I saw this talent walking around the campus that everyone was blind to," Bob recalls. He asked to be named Jackie's primary coach.

Jackie loved basketball, but track and field became more important.

"Either I coached her in the hurdles, long jump, and multi[-sport] events, or I'd quit," Bob threatened the head track coach. "To go on as she had would be an abuse of her talent. Another bad year and she'd go concentrate on basketball, which I considered a waste. Women's basketball careers just come to a stop after college."

Bob got his way. By the fall of 1981, Bob Kersee was in charge of Jackie's training. Although she continued to play basketball, Jackie put more energy into track.

Jackie wanted to focus on her specialty—the long jump. But Bob persuaded her to train for the seven-part heptathlon (which includes the five events of the pentathlon, plus the javelin throw and the 200-meter race). With discipline and the proper training, Bob believed, Jackie could be the best heptathlete in the world.

Bob Kersee challenged Jackie to make the most of her athletic talent.

"He was always yelling, telling me I was lazy and that I had a lot of talent but that I had to give it time to develop," Jackie remembers. "I saw that he was bringing out the best in me." By 1982 Jackie had led the UCLA women's track team to a national championship. She was the best college heptathlete in the country.

In the summer of 1983, Jackie traveled to the Track and Field World Championships in Helsinki, Finland. The best heptathletes of all, the Eastern European women, would be in Helsinki. There, Jackie would face the stiffest competition of her career.

Al Joyner entered the 1983 World Championships too, competing in the triple jump. Jackie and Al cheered for one another. But they walked away from the World Championships without medals. In fact, both Jackie and Al pulled hamstrings during the contest. Al came in eighth in his event. Jackie couldn't even finish the heptathlon because of her injury. "Jackie," Al told his sister, "it's just not our time yet."

Jackie was disappointed. But she had one reason to be happy. Al was moving to Los Angeles. Bob Kersee would coach both of the Joyners in preparation for the upcoming Olympic Games. Their time would come.

The 1984 Olympics were just a year away. Jackie cut back her course load at school and took a break from basketball so she could concentrate on track.

Bob makes sure that Jackie stays healthy and in top condition.

She trained six hours each day—practicing the seven events of the heptathlon: shot put, javelin throw, long jump, high jump, 100-meter hurdles, and 200- and 800-meter runs. She did endurance runs and worked out with weights.

Not even chronic asthma, diagnosed in late 1983, could slow Jackie down. She treated the respiratory condition with a series of medicines, and she trained indoors on smoggy days. By August 1984, she was ready.

Jackie makes leaping over hurdles look easy!

4

Lucky Seven

The 1984 Summer Olympics were held in Los Angeles—which was now home turf for both Jackie and Al Joyner. Al was on the U.S. triple jump team. Jackie was looking for a gold medal in the heptathlon.

In most track-and-field events, the athlete with the fastest time, the highest jump, or the farthest throw is awarded a gold medal. Naming heptathlon winners is not as simple. Officials use a complex math equation that turns an athlete's finishing time or distance in each event into a certain number of points. Point totals from each event are then combined, and the competitor with the highest total score wins the heptathlon. If you added together Jackie's all-time best performances in each of the seven events, she had one of the highest heptathlon point totals in the world.

But the Olympics doesn't take place on paper. Jackie's personal bests meant nothing if she couldn't perform well when the pressure was on. She had to be in top shape for all seven events—scheduled for August 3 and 4, 1984. If she fell short in one category, she could try to make up points by posting high scores in the events that followed.

Jackie came to the Games with confidence. By the end of the first day of competition, she held a sizable lead over the field of heptathletes.

But the next day did not go as well. A sore hamstring hobbled Jackie in the long jump and cut into her lead. Coming into the last event, the 800-meter run, Australia's Glynis Nunn was within striking distance. Still, if Jackie could stay close to Nunn in the exhausting race, she'd earn enough points to win the gold medal.

As the 800 progressed, Nunn moved to the front of the pack and Jackie gave chase. Al, watching from the infield along the track, screamed at his sister to run faster. "Pump your arms, Jackie!" he shouted, "This is it!"

Jackie surged to the finish line behind Nunn. But her time was not good enough. When the final point totals were tallied, Nunn posted 6,390 points to Jackie's 6,385.

Jackie was devastated. She had lost the gold medal by a tiny margin.

A poor showing in just one heptathlon event can cost an athlete the whole contest.

Many people blamed the loss on Jackie's sore hamstring. But, "it wasn't an injury that cost me the gold medal," Jackie insisted, "it was my mentality....I doubted my capabilities. I never thought in positive terms about what it was going to take...to come across the finish line first or to come across doing my best."

Al Joyner sprints toward the takeoff mark in the triple jump. He will then take a hop, a stride, and a jump into the sand pit.

"Negative thoughts were filling her head," Bob Kersee added. "They turned gold into silver."

Jackie's disappointment was offset by her brother's showing in the triple jump, though. Al hadn't been expected to win a medal. Yet he had won the gold!

After his victory, Al met up with Jackie at the heptathlon medal ceremony. Tears streamed down her face as she accepted the silver medal. "It's okay," Al said, comforting his sister on her second-place finish. "It's okay."

"I'm not crying because I lost," Jackie told her brother. "I'm crying because you won. You fooled them all."

After the Olympics, Jackie returned to UCLA to finish her bachelor's degree in history and communications. She played basketball again and resumed heptathlon training. The long jump was Jackie's flagship event. In 1985 she set an American record with a jump of 23 feet, 9 inches.

Meanwhile, her friendship with Bob Kersee grew deeper. "We could talk about absolutely anything," Jackie recalls. "And whatever acclaim came to me didn't bother him."

Bob and Jackie had been working together for four years. Slowly, friendship turned into romance. Bob proposed to Jackie at a Houston Astros baseball game in the summer of 1985. On January 11, 1986, Jackie and Bob were married.

Jackie clears the high jump bar with ease.

They don't call it the long jump for nothing!

The 1988 Olympics were two years off. But Jackie was eager to take another crack at a gold medal. She trained full-time. Bob, now husband and coach to Jackie, worked harder than ever too. He trained student athletes at UCLA and worked privately coaching Jackie and other Olympic hopefuls.

Meanwhile, Jackie's personal bests in the heptathlon events kept climbing. The world record, held by Sabine Paetz of East Germany, stood at 6,946 points. Jackie knew she could break it.

She wouldn't have to wait very long. In July 1986, at the Goodwill Games in Moscow, Russia, Jackie ran, jumped, and threw like a superwoman. When the meet ended, Jackie had set six personal bests. She had piled up 7,148 points—shattering the world heptathlon record by more than 200!

Other athletes were shocked. "No way you're ever going to do *that* again," high jumper Dwight Stones told Jackie when he heard about her accomplishment. But less than a month later, at the United States Olympic Festival in Houston, Texas, Jackie did it again.

She ran away with the heptathlon, racking up 7,161 points. Her nearest competitor was more than 1,000 points behind! Jackie was thrilled. "It happened in the United States in front of the people I know," she said. "That's a good feeling."

Each year the AAU gives the Sullivan Memorial Trophy to the nation's most outstanding amateur athlete. The list of past winners includes great champions such as decathlete Bruce Jenner, track legend Carl Lewis, and diver Greg Louganis. The winner for 1986 was easy to choose: Jackie Joyner-Kersee.

Jackie accepts the prestigious Sullivan Award.

5

Gold Fever

"I'm expecting two golds and two world records," Bob Kersee told Jackie before their trip to the 1988 Olympic Games in Seoul, South Korea. "When I go to Seoul," Jackie told reporters, "I'm going to be hungry."

Bob and Jackie's expectations were well founded. At the Olympic Trials in Indianapolis in July, Jackie had upped her own world record in the heptathlon to 7,215 points.

So, no one was very surprised when Jackie topped the record again—for the fourth time in two years—with a score of 7,291 in Seoul. No one flinched when she nailed a personal heptathlon best in the long jump and ripped through the 800 meters in record time to win the gold medal.

The high jump has its ups and downs!

Jackie's nearest opponent, Sabine John of East Germany, finished almost 400 points behind to take the silver. "Let's face it," Bob said, "[Jackie] has only been competing against herself in the heptathlon for the last three years."

A week later, Jackie grabbed her second gold medal of the Games, beating another East German, Heike Drechsler, with a 24-foot, 3½-inch long jump— an Olympic record. The long jump was Jackie's only individual event. But she might have put a scare into the world's best high jumpers, throwers, hurdlers, and runners, had she entered more individual competitions.

"She's on another planet," marveled U.S. teammate Cindy Greiner. "If Jackie wants to work at it, I think she's capable of setting world records, individually, in six of the seven events."

How could Jackie excel in so many track-and-field events at once? "There are going to be good competitors in each event," Jackie explained, "so I prepare to go against the best in each event. I want to win each event. And if I do that, then the scoring totals will take care of themselves."

"She takes one event after another as if each were for the gold medal," Bob added. "She is capable of sustaining that level of intensity throughout two days."

Jackie could have focused on one event like other athletes do. She would most likely have broken the world record in the long jump had she not scattered her energy in seven different directions. But Jackie prefers a tough challenge. "I like the heptathlon," she said, "because it shows you what you're made of."

Jackie was a popular athlete at the 1988 Games. The media and the fans flocked around her. But, despite Jackie's accomplishments, another Joyner captured even more attention. She was fast and she was flashy. She was Jackie's sister-in-law—sprinter Florence Griffith Joyner.

Like Jackie, Florence Griffith had trained under Bob Kersee at UCLA. There, Florence met Al Joyner, whom she married a few years later.

Florence Griffith Joyner was the darling of the 1988 Summer Games. She ran in Day-Glo bodysuits—sometimes with one legging cut off the outfit. She sported long, painted fingernails and flowing black curls. And no one was faster. By the end of the Games, "Flo Jo" had captured one silver and three gold medals.

Jackie was quiet and simple. Photogenic Flo Jo turned heads wherever she went. But Jackie didn't resent her sister-in-law's fame. There was no rivalry between the two athletes. Nor was there ill will after the Olympic Trials, when Florence announced that Al, not Bob, would coach her in Seoul. "We are family," Jackie said. "We all love each other. And that's more important than gold medals."

Jackie's sister-in-law Flo Jo made a big splash in Seoul.

Jackie had many reasons to be happy in Seoul. But her spirits sank when a Brazilian runner, Joaquin Cruz, spread a cruel rumor. Cruz said that Jackie and Flo Jo had used performance-enhancing drugs called steroids.

The accusation upset Jackie. "I worked hard to get to where I am," she told reporters, "and I haven't used drugs to do it."

Dedication combined with natural talent has made Jackie a champion.

Jackie hated drug use. In East St. Louis, she had seen many lives hurt by drug and alcohol abuse. The only drugs Jackie ever used were asthma medicines, prescribed by a doctor.

"I've never thought about taking drugs," she remarked. "I see what they have done to other people. . . . I won't even take a drink."

Top athletes are routinely tested for illegal drug use, and Jackie and Flo Jo came up clean on every test. Cruz was criticized for his remarks, and the rumors about steroids quickly vanished.

When Jackie returned to Los Angeles, she was asked to advertise products and appear on television talk shows. The Women's Sports Foundation named Jackie its Amateur Athlete of the Year for the second year in a row. The *Sporting News* named Jackie "Woman of the Year" as the outstanding athlete of 1988. The paper had named only "Men of the Year" since creating the award in 1968. Jackie was the first woman and the first track-and-field athlete to win the newspaper's top honor. She was a groundbreaker.

The shot put (above) and the javelin require great upper-body strength.

6
Home Stretch

Athletics hasn't been the only job on Jackie's mind. She has always tried to do positive work off the field as well. Jackie is famous and earns a lot of money endorsing products for companies such as Nike, Honda, and Glaxo Wellcome (asthma medication). Jackie uses her good fortune to help others, especially disadvantaged kids in her old hometown. "The most important thing was . . . being able to go back to East St. Louis," Jackie explained, "and let the young people see those medals and show that hard work pays off."

With Bob's help, Jackie established the Jackie Joyner-Kersee Community Foundation as a means of helping young people in poor urban communities.

Jackie donates a portion of every dollar that she earns to the foundation.

Much of the foundation's work has focused on making East St. Louis a better place to live. "East St. Louis has been called a bad place," Jackie says. "But I feel that there are a lot of people here who care about human beings being human. All we need to do is to get together, and we can become a great city."

The Jackie Joyner-Kersee Foundation has taken on a number of projects. The organization pays for young athletes from East St. Louis and other poor communities to go to the Junior Olympics. The effort is near to Jackie's heart.

"There were people, when I was little, reaching into their pockets trying to make sure I could go to the Junior Olympics, trying to make things possible for me. I feel that in return I can do that for the next generation. . . . I hope I can inspire someone to take the right path and be successful."

In November 1988, Jackie and Bob took 100 children from East St. Louis to New York City for the annual Macy's Thanksgiving Day Parade. Most of the kids had never left their hometown before. The plane trip to New York showed the youngsters an exciting new world.

Jackie also travels across the country, giving speeches to groups of young people. One of her strongest messages is about staying away from drugs.

Jackie will continue to work to increase the popularity of track and field even after her retirement.

"I . . . believe it is the responsibility of Olympic champions to give something back to our youth, to the public," she says. "It's our duty."

In the 1992 Olympics, Jackie won a gold medal in the heptathlon and a bronze in the long jump. Once again "the World's Greatest Athlete" was all over the news. Jackie wanted to compete in the Olympics one more time—in Atlanta, Georgia. "I want to finish on American soil in 1996," she said. "It would be a dream come true for me. That's where my motivation comes from."

Arriving in Atlanta with a hamstring injury, Jackie approached the heptathlon with her usual determination. Bob, of course, was with her. Jackie once said, "On the athletic field, Bobby looks at me as an athlete and not as his wife." This unique relationship has been tough, especially when Jackie was hurt. Bob has said that "as soon as the husband starts to worry: 'That's my wife out there in pain,' the coach has to say [to the husband]: 'Shut up and get back in the stands.'"

However, in the Atlanta Olympics, the husband overruled the coach. After watching Jackie struggle in pain with the hurdles and the high jump, Bob pulled her from the heptathlon. A few days later, Jackie returned to compete in the long jump. Although her leg was still injured, her strong spirit and the support of the crowd helped her win the bronze medal. The third-place award felt like a gold medal to Jackie because she hadn't given up, even when things were going badly. She had made her mark in her final Olympics.

Later that year, Jackie returned to a sport she hadn't played since college when she played briefly for the Richmond Rage of the American Basketball League. Although her return to the court was short-lived, she had the experience of once again being a team player rather than an individual competitor.

Bob and Jackie share a laugh during a warmup session.

Jackie takes a victory lap at the Olympic Trials in New Orleans.

Jackie also tried publishing in 1997. That year she co-authored her life story, which is titled *A Kind of Grace*.

Jackie decided to retire from competition in 1998. But first, she wanted to compete in a final Goodwill Games. Since the Games began in 1986, she had won every Goodwill heptathlon. In July 1998, she once again won the event in New York City for her final victory on American soil. Jackie's last track-and-field event was a farewell long jump in Edwardsville, Illinois, near her hometown of East St. Louis. After that, she retired at age 36, still holding the heptathlon world record.

Jackie's career opened doors for females in sports. She plans to keep working for fairness in athletics as well as continuing to promote track and field and share her good fortune with others.

As head of Elite International Sports Marketing, Jackie will remain a role model and a major influence in the sports world. Elite manages Jackie's endorsements as well as representing other athletes from track and field and other sports. Jackie's foundation will also keep her busy. One of its major goals is building a youth center in her hometown.

When not juggling her many public activities, Jackie likes to relax at home with Bob. Jackie and Bob hope to have children. They are also active in their church. In addition to coaching, Bob is a minister, and Jackie became a born-again Christian in 1985.

Jackie and Bob were deeply saddened in September 1998 when Florence Griffith Joyner died. Jackie's colorful and talented sister-in-law died unexpectedly in her sleep of a brain disorder.

At work or at home, Jackie never stops setting new goals and taking on new challenges. She is living proof that hard work and positive thinking can turn dreams into reality. "I have a philosophy based on the 'three Ds': desire, dedication, and determination," she explains. "If you want to be successful in anything, you must have discipline. You have to set goals and then accomplish them."

At the 1987 Pan American Games in Indianapolis, Jackie ties the world long jump record with a 24-foot, 5½-inch jump.

JACKIE JOYNER-KERSEE'S HEPTATHLON STATISTICS

Gold Medal Performances

Event	*Seoul Olympics* September 1988 (world record)		*Barcelona Olympics* August 1992	
	Performance	Points	Performance	Points
100 METER HURDLES	12.69 sec.	1172	12.85 sec.	1147
HIGH JUMP	6 ft., 1¼ in.	1054	6 ft., 3¼ in.	1119
SHOT PUT	51 ft., 10 in.	915	46 ft., 4¼ in.	803
200 METERS	22.56 sec.	1123	23.12 sec.	1067
LONG JUMP	23 ft., 10¼ in.	1264	23 ft., 3½ in.	1206
JAVELIN	149 ft., 10 in.	776	147 ft., 7 in.	763
800 METERS	2 min., 8.51 sec.	987	2 min., 11.78 sec.	939
Total		7291		7044

Personal Bests

Event	Place	Date	Performance	Points
100 METER HURDLES	San Jose, Cal.	June 1988	12.61 sec.	1184
HIGH JUMP	Indianapolis, Ind.	July 1988	6 ft., 4 in.	1145
SHOT PUT	Irvine, Cal.	June 1988	55 ft., 3 in.	985
200 METERS	Indianapolis, Ind.	July 1988	22.30 sec.	1150
LONG JUMP	New York, N.Y.	May 1994	24 ft., 7 in.	1341
JAVELIN	Houston, Tex.	August 1986	164 ft., 5 in.	862
800 METERS	Seoul, S. Korea	September 1988	2 min., 8.51 sec.	987
Total				7654

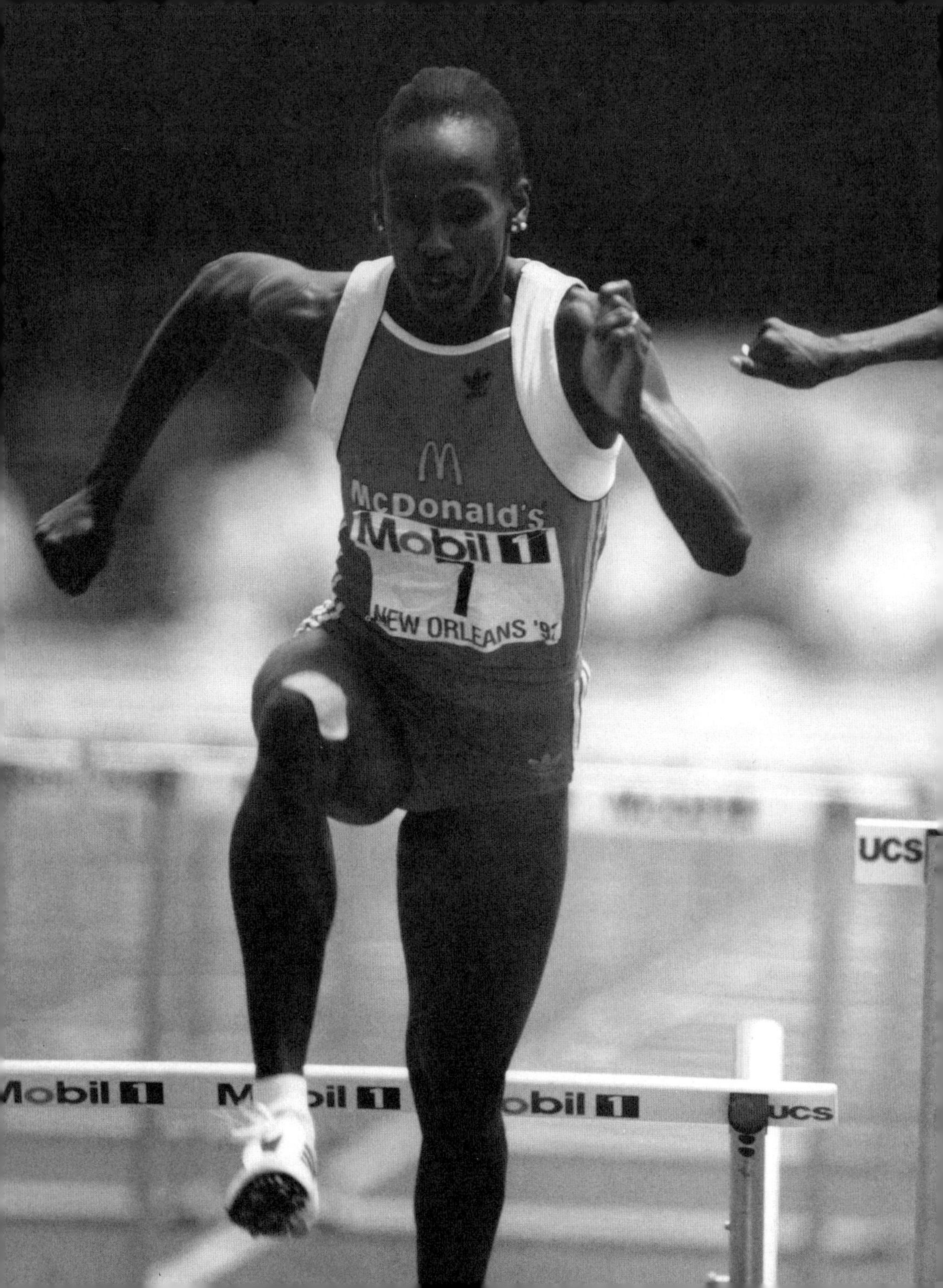
McDonald's
Mobil 1
7
UCS

ABOUT THE AUTHORS

Margaret J. Goldstein was born in Detroit and graduated from the University of Michigan. She is the author of several books for young readers, including *Brett Hull: Hockey's Top Gun* and *Jennifer Capriati: Tennis Sensation.*

Jennifer Larson was a seven-time All American in track and cross-country at St. Olaf College in Northfield, Minnesota. She works as a children's book editor and lives in St. Paul.

ACKNOWLEDGMENTS

Photographs reproduced with permission of Mary Ann Carter, pp. 1, 27, 36, 38, 47, 49, 53; SportsChrome East/West (Robert Tringali Jr.), pp. 2, 9, 28, 34 (top and bottom), 41, 42, 44; John Biever, pp. 6, 10, 31, 50, 55; SportsChrome East/West (Eileen Langsley), p. 11; Lincoln High School, p. 12; Jackie Joyner-Kersee, p. 17; UCLA Sports Information Department, pp. 20, 22, 24, 25; Arkansas State University, p. 32. Front cover: SportsChrome East/West (Louis A. Raynor); back cover: SportsChrome East/West (Robert Tringali Jr.).